Navigational Problems

Elisavietta Ritchie and Donald Grady Shomette

The Wineberry Press
Solomons, Maryland
2020

Copyright 2020 ©
by The Wineberry Press

All rights reserved, including the right to reproduce this book or portions thereof in any form or by any means, electronic or mechanical, including photocopying, recording, or by any information storage and retrieval system, without permission in writing from the publisher, Solomons, Maryland

Book design and photgraphs by Donald Grady Shomette

Printed in the United States of America

FIRST EDITION

Library of Congress Cataloging-in-Publication Data

Navigational Problems 1st. ed.

Includes poetry, photographs and illustrative matter

ISBN. 978-1-7332326-1-6.

1. Poetry. Ritchie, Elisavietta

CONTENTS

2	Prefigurations
3	Dissecting and Orange
4	Navigational Hazards
5	On Weathering Gales
6	Oolong in the Storm
7	Swimmer
8	Ours Is an Untidy Earth
9	Seaward
10	Flotsam, Jetsam
11	Moon Pursuit
12	Eternal as Turtles
13	Wineberries
14	Stealing Blackberries on Broomes Island
15	Real Toads
16	Transmissions
17	Beyond the North Woods
18	Osprey
19	The Heron Has Landed
20	Siren Summer
21	Tasting the Names
22	A Circle of Stones
23	A Gift of Sea Shells
24	Forces, Voices
25	A Japanese Morning
26	Bathers, Dunningford Cove
27	Memento
28	For a Clinical Survey Inquiring About First Loves
29	You Ask If I've Met The Famous Writer
30	Proprietary Codes
31	Company
32	Occupation: Aviator
33	Directions to the Boat
34	Amanda Contemplates the Duck Blind
35	Infolding
36	Conjectures In a Small Cemetery Beyond the No-Frills Microtel
37	The Saint in a Box of Glass
38	Fire Works: Chronicles from a War
39	Forget I Gave You Ancestors to Die For
40	Luckies Taste Good!
41	For a Certain Poet in Prison
42	Night Shift
43	Existential Questions
44	Visions of My Half-Awake
45	Tidal Questions
46	Case Histories: You Say I Am Now One
47	Choreography
48	*About Authors*

PREFIGURATIONS

in one wide tree
he sees a boat

in milkweed seeds
the billowed sails

in stones the earth
in ponds the sea

in puddles sky
in candles stars

and in one heart
unchartered waterways

TO DISSECT AN ORANGE
Advice for a young poet

Consider orange peels tonight
Focus on your six imperfect trapezoids,
two wheels of cut-off ends. The underface of white
is edible, pick off the strings. Avoid

the heart, a tasteless pith like twist of paper towel.
Inside the tiny ovoid cylinders,
flesh quivers, waits. Don't muse aloud
on Orange as Obvious Metaphor.
Check out the color, scent, the feel and taste
of juice that coats your hands, your smile,
your Sunday shirt. Oranges kill a cold with haste
and keep you from starvation for a while.

Play with details. Do more than just describe.
Cut excess words—but keep essential adjectives this time.
What philosophic value to the exercise? Divine.
(A modifier or imperative?) Ditch rhyme.

Next, eat the orange. What's left? Fling
detritus in the compost bin atop the weeds
for possum and raccoon. Come spring,
the mulch will fertilize five sprouting ivory seeds.

Now wash.

NAVIGATIONAL HAZARDS

I never warned you: falling in love is not
as simple as tumbling from a canoe
in shallow coves and donning new jeans
as if nothing changed.

Sand and mud, water bugs, seaweed strands cling.
Crabs snatch out your sun-struck eyes.
Minnows of lust keep nibbling bared flesh.
Electric or moray, sea-serpents bite.

Ebb tide can pull you into strange seas
or leave you ship-wrecked, thirsty, deranged . . .
No matter how leaky the battered hull,
we still steer into the next hurricane.

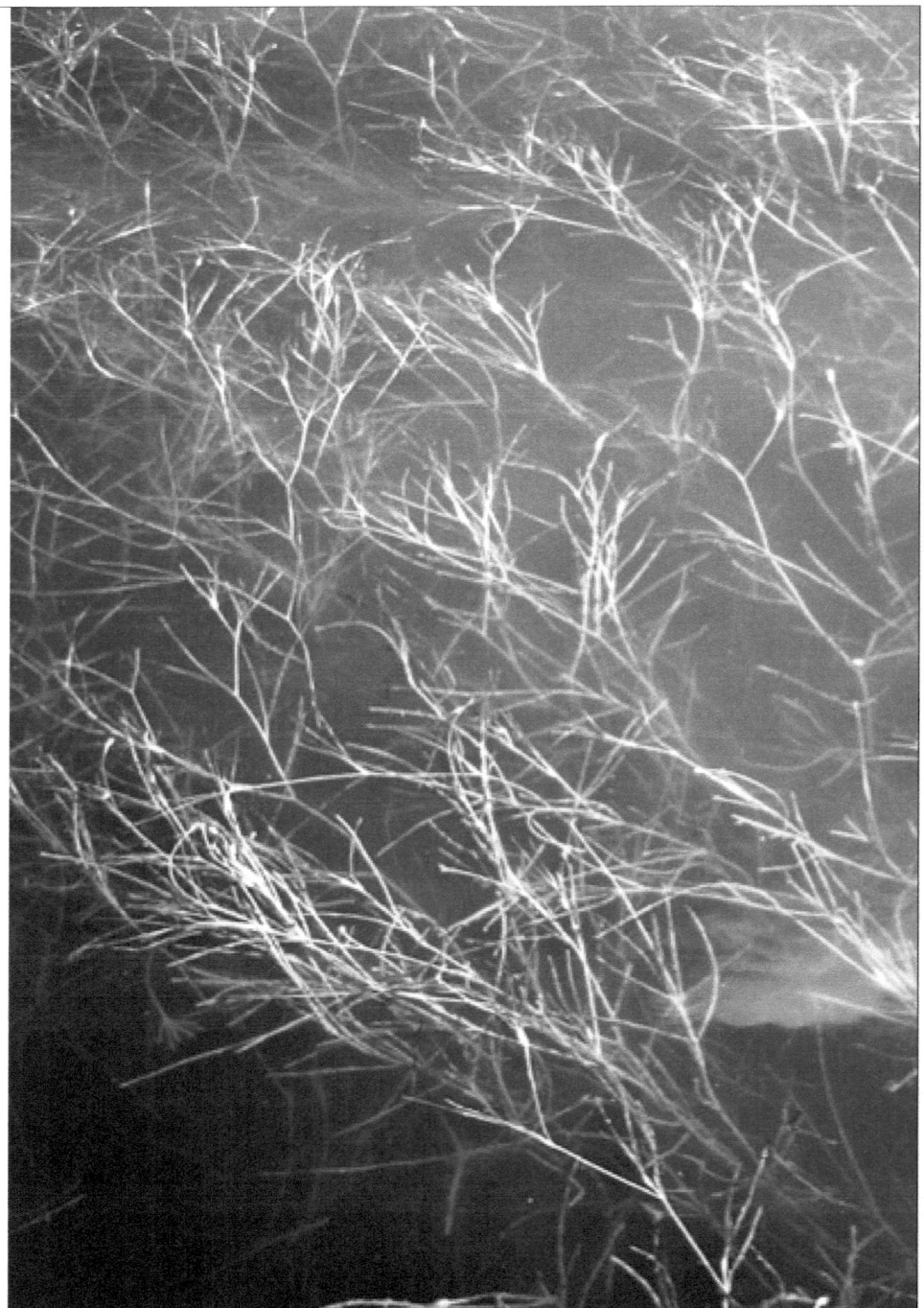

ON WEATHERING GALES

Whether to rig the sea anchor
from stem or from stern
depends on the cut of the hull.

If the line is streamed from the bow
the boat may lie broadside to waves
or make sternway too fast, jam the rudder.

If you rig from the stern, following seas
can flood the cockpit—you'll swamp.
In either case, tow ropes chafe, fray and break.

Run for port—assuming you know where
you are on the chart. Risk going aground,
or smashing up at the lighthouse.

Mainsail and mizzen are reefed.
You heel more with each swell.
Shortening sail is no longer enough.

Then strip the masts,
lash the helm, lie a'hull
in the troughs between crests.

Bare poles respond to the wind.
You heave and reach on through the seas.
Perhaps you can ride out the night.

The question is, why
are you out here at all?
Yet you know:

As soon as you're dry and repaired
you'll set sail again,
still stalking the perfect wind.

OOLONG IN THE STORM

Let smoky Oolong tea and raisins soaked in rum
remind us both of ancient loves and current pains . . .

We're trapped inside one huge aquarium!

Rain *is* cascading down these walls of glass, rain
and more rain.

The radio reports flood warnings out.
Look, tide fills up the cove, then does not drain.

Just the usual wet spring.

Can half a moon, unseen beyond
the storm, grab the helm
of tides and pull them back?

Come on, let's splash through puddles, ponds,
to gauge if surf might overwhelm
the bulkhead, drown the yard again.

Should we not dump the tea and save
books, photos, manuscripts, the cat?
She scratches at the door and cries.
We'd best grab everything, pack up and run.

And leave half-written joys and troubles lovers gave
in those forgotten months of drought?

The whole wall's cracked!

Why be wise?
Let's boil more tea, and take another chance,
gamble on the drying power of the sun.

You think wrecked hearts can heal enough to fancy
one more fling . . .

SWIMMER

The waters are slipping away from you
or you are slipping into the waters.
You stayed on shore as long as you could,

or, changing the mermaid's story,
you had sung long enough
and the surf no longer frightened,

so you decided: time now to dive.
You already know your own voice.
You were never afraid of the deeps.

You will re-enter as specks, scales
of the tiniest minnows or mermaids,
diatoms caught in sun rays, diffusing in blue.

This is the way to swim.
I also will learn the currents.
Teach me the path to the beach.

1. OURS IS AN UNTIDY EARTH

I have known hurricanes
mostly those that broke
in another time or state
somewhere up the coast

and, first hand, one that surged
over bulkheads, covered lawn,
flooded woods, crept up steps—
surf beat all night against our house.

Flood swamped the car, stored gear
and water pump. Still, our power worked.
Creatures reached the higher slopes,
most wrecked terrain regrows.

Yet I know those other coasts
tropic and exotic,
roadless and unchartered,
awash with people and heat.

Now that sea inscribes its own
trajectory, leaving new
rivers, gullies, mounts and maps,
unnamed orphans, nameless mounds.

Did all the gods conspire
for this terrible housecleaning?
Gods are a capricious lot. Even here,
the drowned keep tapping at our windowpane.

2. MORE TSUNAMI NEWS

Those unknown women noted only afterward
who did not, could not, flee the wave
poised like Hokusai's above the boat,
the home, the fields, the street, the beach

where children played, turned to snatch them up,
then rushed already burdened with the kettle, pot,
ancestral portraits, best batiks, half-made bread,
items women think about.

They did not make it,
while their men, who farmed higher ground
or rode out the strangely buoyant seas
or faster, just outran the waves, mostly survived . . .

A curl of surf in every sea.

SEAWARD

I used to dream their sweeping past
slipped from my grasp
in the shroud of the night.

This hot October afternoon
three semi-circles of curl
curve in the tide,

ride seaward with leaves
on maiden and final journeys
fog-bound, bay-bound, ocean-bound.

Autumnal aurelias float past my line,
a question mark which asks
forgiveness of the final fish.

The tide quickens, stealing
my children seaward with leaves—
My crabnet can't retrieve them now—

Nor my cast line.
Around the channel buoy
a shark fin splits the harbor's rind.

FLOTSAM, JETSAM

Translucent medusas in the surf
surf heaps medusas on the beach
surf tumbles agates milky as cataracts
tumbles a body in the waves

always one washes in at our feet
boulders sharp with barnacles and crabs
jut from surf at low tide
yet the body shows no scrapes

a shift of light at the edge of beach
at night the body emits a gleam
of phosphorus while it decays
glowworms of the soul burn our brains

what sense   could this be that corpse
in the stranger's dream   an armored
knight she recalled   rolled in by the surf
from holes in his mask a terrible light

or is this be the one on the isle *I saw my first
corpse at fifteen* read the young girl's diary   *the day
after I lost my virginity for the first time
he'd been in the sea three weeks*

awake for years to find how to read
the message in surf and stanzas on sand
what strewn flotsam means
how did he die   why find him here in the sea

again and again   awake or in dreams
what do we do with the dead
like a mouse on Limoges gold-rimmed green
what do we do with the light

MOON PURSUIT

To get a jump on the moon
I swam out where it would rise
this night most close to Earth.

I treaded water on top of that place,
felt boiling beneath
my pale churning legs.

A turtle emerged, sifting foam,
I lunged, grabbed his shell—
He tried to bite.

I braided my hair, reined him in,
but he swam the horizon with me
weaving seines with the wake of his plunge.

"Please! Let's return! The moon
will soon rise!" Out there, the sea swelled.
The moon crowned, huge, tearing waves.

We thrashed across crests. The apricot slid up the sky
"Quick! It will turn into ice!"
He stretched his neck long, spread his beak

and caught the moon right in his jaws,
chomped them shut, dripping blood.
We swam home in the dark.

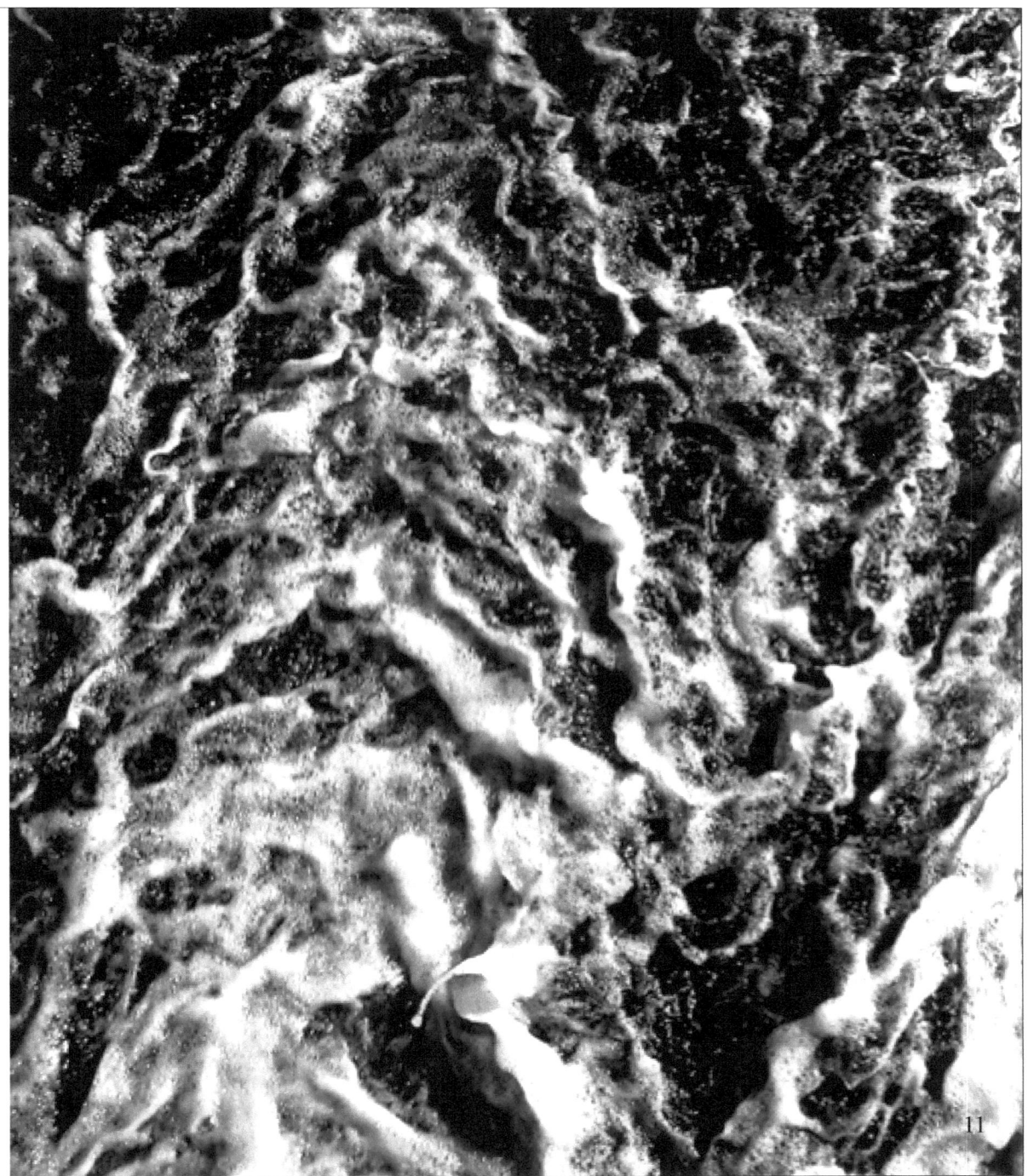

ETERNAL AS TURTLES

So we
          are forced
 to court
         slowly
 sharing
          fallen persimmons
and swollen berries
           with care
  to probe
     deep beneath shells
 where the skin
    above the heart
and other vital parts
        is not
  so impregnable
     and to bear
 our impenetrable
        love
everywhere.

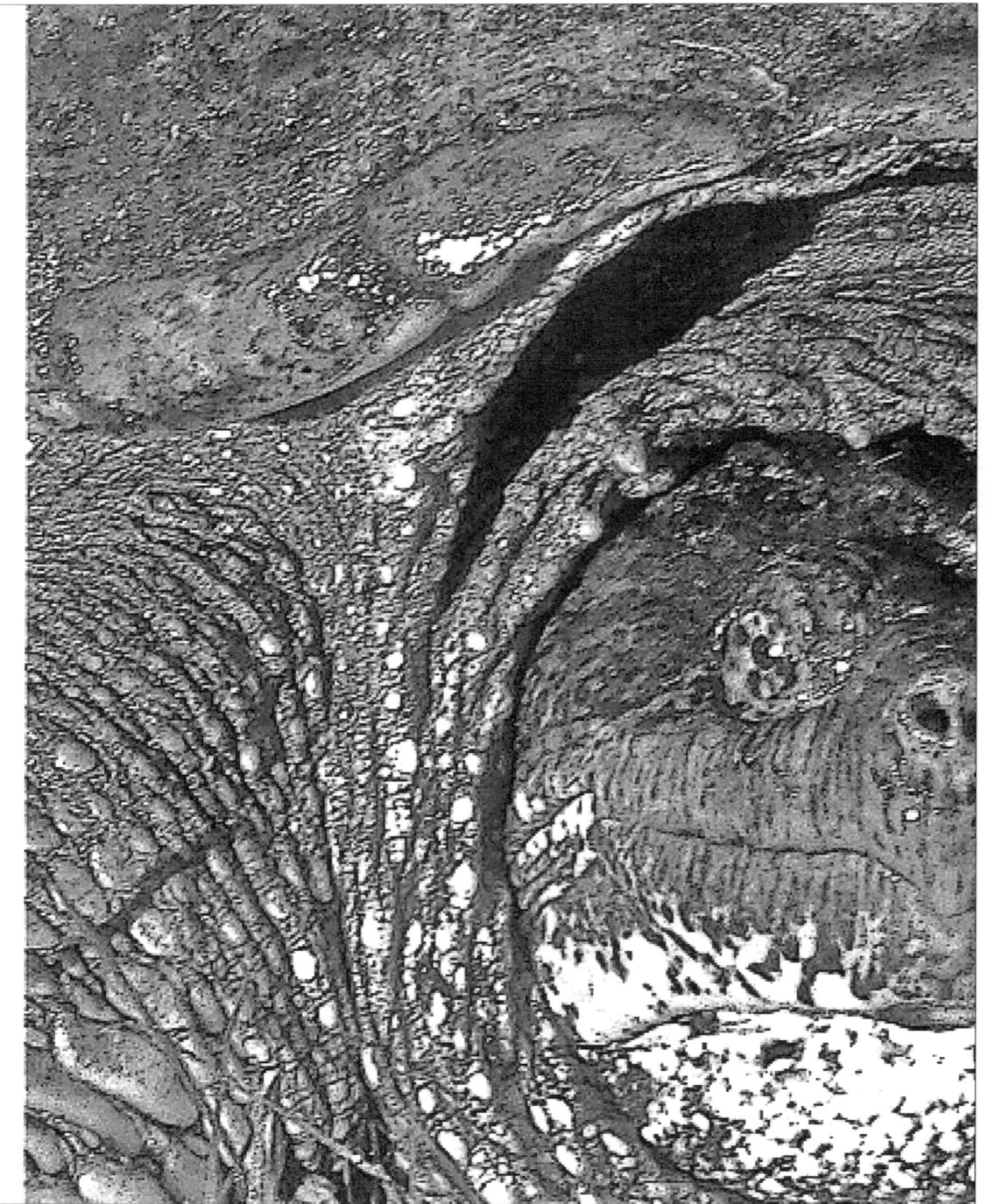

WINEBERRIES

1.
Our lips are bruised with berries,
our fingers pricked by thorns,
but the fruit stays pale and tart.

Still, stained with juice and blood
and hidden by the vines:
one dark kiss before we part.

This week while we are gone
the berries redden to their prime.
Mourning doves, box turtles,

woodchucks gorge themselves maroon,
coordinating hunger, ripeness and the time
as we cannot.

2.
To find the berries of forgetfulness
Great Uncle Ramsey picked his way
across the fields whose furrows burst
soy beans, corn, alfalfa, wheat, jimson weed,
misplaced arrowheads and oyster shells,

to reach the woods, where at the edge
of tangled briars and poison ivy, trumpet vines,
morning glory, bella donna, foxes' dens.
Here berries reddened and turned sweet.
Not bucketfuls. That was a woman's work.

He merely chose the ripest fruit.
When he returned at last, unsteady
but serene, he could not remember where
he'd been, Paris, London or New York?
But he had dined with kings.

STEALING BLACKBERRIES ON BROOMES ISLAND

I kayak to the swatch of sand to wrest the berries—ripe, big
as thumbs—from barbarous thorns and vigilant wasps.
First check no one's around.

This farm four-centuries-old *was* mine, and though I wander far,
remains my soul's terrain. A misplaced Slav dares speak
of *soul* and *terra irredentta*.

Beside the sea, two hidden ponds, bean fields, nut trees, barn,
chicken house and a stable big enough for a troika,
a proper *dacha* for nobility down on its luck:

roofs leaked, walls mossed, floors creaked, a prehistoric furnace spewed
cinders, soot and chimney swifts. The landlord had bought it cheap
from dying farmers, rented dear, swore *No Repairs*.

We paid, scrubbed muck, painted walls gloss white, high ceilings blue,
doors red for royalty. We planted basil, artichokes, asparagus,
Great Aunt Eugenya's grave,

and hosted insect kingdoms, dynasties of ferral cats, black snakes,
proprietary mice, and gangly vulture chicks,
strayed princes, poets, lovers, tramps.

I gleaned berries from a grove until the landlord chased
the foxes out, cut trees, ground stumps, uprooted berry canes.
Next, he reclaimed the farm.

Like Genghis Khan, he trashed both house and barn, plowed
our gardens under, bared the fields, departed, returned.
Now he's burned the whole place down.

Yet this July, new bushes swathe the farm, weeds veil the fields,
charred cellars and smashed chimneys. And look—
the briars produce *huge berries no one's picked*.

Crouched at high tide, one hour and my bucket's full,
hands and face are purple-black.
A petty theft? I felt no guilt.

*His crime site veiled, the noble house survives. Wisteria wreathes
the stones, scarlet trumpet vines crown trees. Hummingbirds
and luna moths and stags—Everything and everyone alive.*

How sweet are berries fed on ash and blood! Preserved in vodka, some
warm winter's wakes, the revels of scorched souls
who still seek lost domains.

REAL TOADS

The real toad in my real
garden has no illusions he
could make it big on the poetry scene.

he lived here last year, or
his mother/brother/uncle/aunt
although one doesn't think of toads

bestowed or cursed with genealogy
or sibling squabbles: who gets the biggest fly?
Green horned tomato hookworms plenty here.

What if he ate a bug poem by mistake?
Choked down sestinas line by line,
dripped rhymes, spat out clichés?

Toad fate depends on weather, and the cats:
Telemachus our tabby used to catch
and gulp toads live, legs dribbled down his chin.

Late 1980's: silence. No toads left in the yard.
Ribets strangely vanished from the world—
a scientific fact: toads even scarce in Africa.

1996, Australia, we found no lack
of leopard frogs or cane toads—
the venom in their spines could kill a cat.

Last winter, digging holes for pansy plants
my trowel unearthed two thumb-sized toads
too soon so I reburied them in mud.

This summer in my garden, my real toad,
grown up, benign, eats bugs, imprints
his syllables on dust, hops out an action poem.

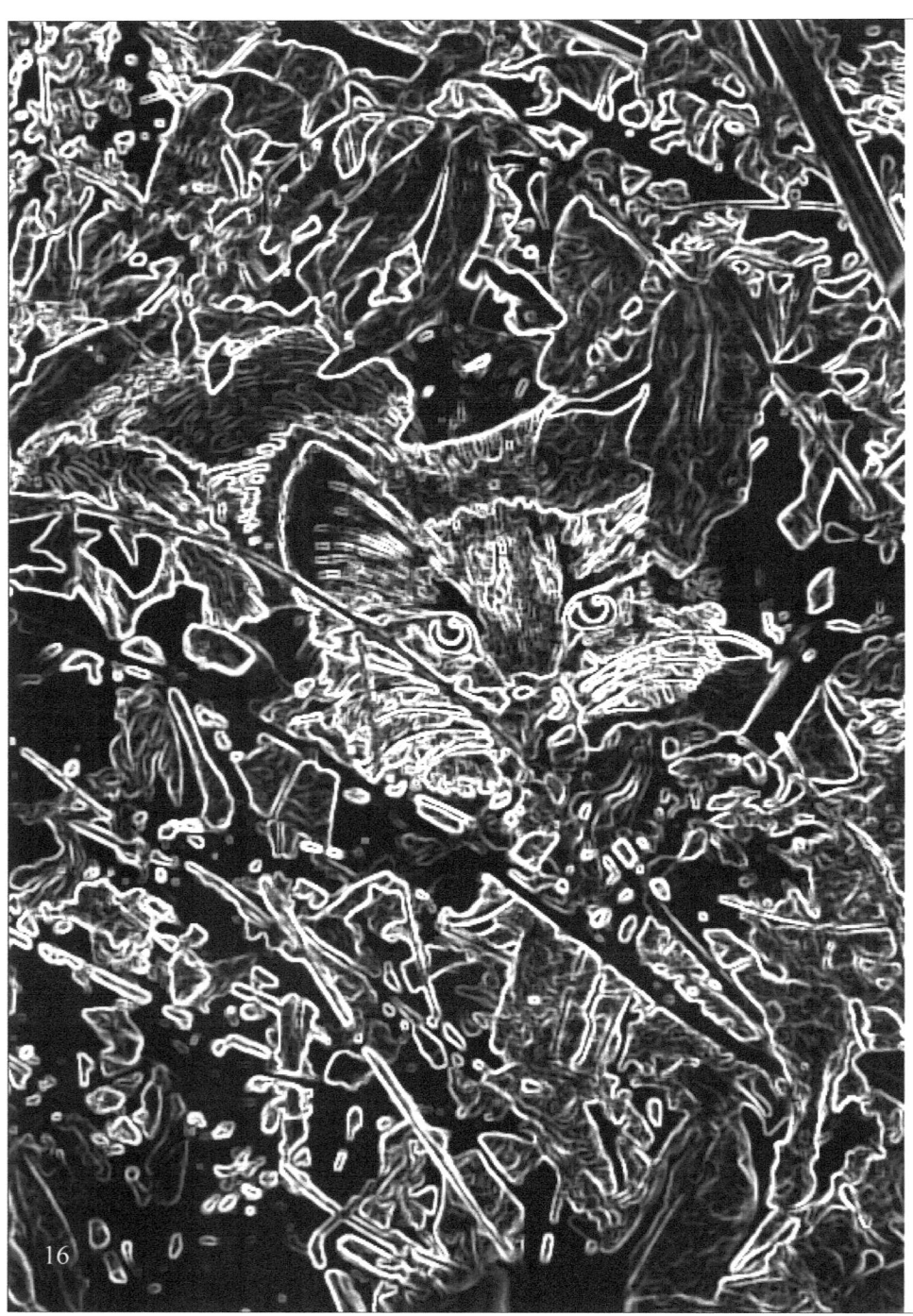

TRANSMISSIONS

At seventeen our black angora cat,
scruffy with leaves and bugs and dirt,

sagged close to the ground—
could he know he'd soon join it?

Paws spread across the stripped towel,
he sprawled all evening just inside

the garden door, sliding glass,
the possum nose-to nose beyond.

Next morning, we dug into the hard field,
planted a monkey pine.

October tenth, a white angora with one green eye,
one blue, escaped a stable across the swamp.

No name, no age, I tried to return her,
but she ate the rest of the tuna.

She'd also lie at garden end. For now
she stays, and picks out her own tree.

BEYOND THE NORTH WOODS

Snow crusts each birch and pine,
branch and log and stump.
The path is gone.

Suddenly a shake
of winter-thickened fur –
a timber wolf.

I freeze as still.
We watch each other.
Snowflakes catch on eyelashes.

Do we both weigh our lives,
a final meal,
a fragile future of pursuit?

A tree cracks like a shot –
crashes –
avalanches snow –

In a flash
we separate
toward different woods.

He will not lose
his way,
or point out mine.

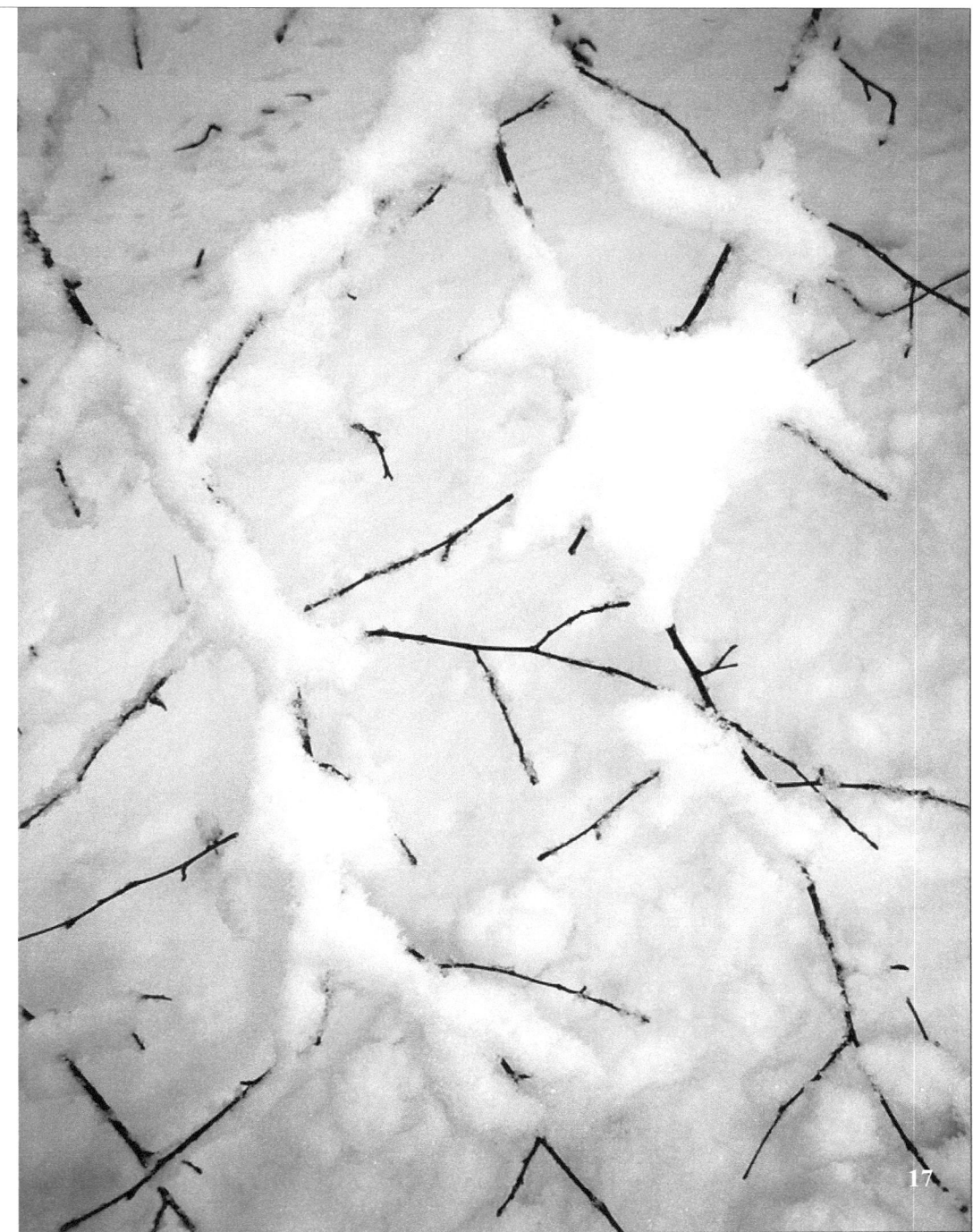

OSPREY

No fabled falcon
trained to wrists
of prince or feudal lord

this fish hawk builds
a scraggly nest of sticks
atop the channel marker

swirled by tides and prey
to floods and hurricanes
the cry a tenor peep

yet when he soars
rides the waves of sky
his shadow knifes the sea

he plummets through
talons his prize
bears it home

THE HERON HAS LANDED

Years I've stalked the heron of the cove
in pre-dawn mist, the late hour of gold

he lands in the shallows, prints
a cryptic alphabet of quicksand, picks

the nymphs of dragonflies
minnows for his silver lunch

the water snake sinews a question mark
his ripples spell circuitous, circuitous   and disappear

he scatters copies of himself
great blue great **blue** great blue

flaps off   till dark I try to catch his croak
can only photograph calligraphies of geese

SIREN SUMMER

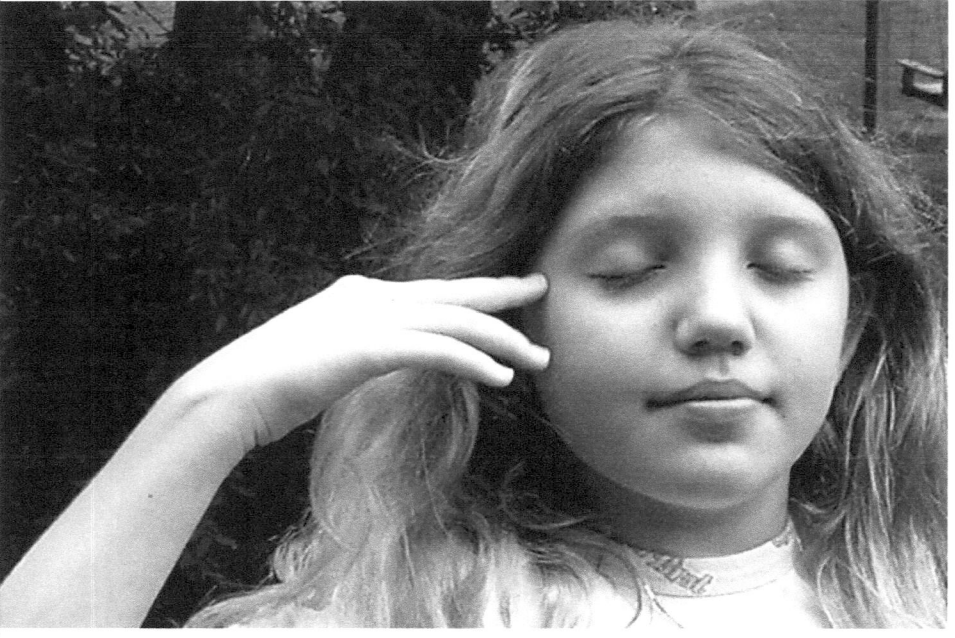

I even then was dreaming of you

summers when on splintered docks
shelling peas beside the waves
a princess still,
my daisy crown askew,

I waited for the curious seaplanes to return,
fly perilously low above my waving arms,
mistake me for grown up,
wave back, wag wings,
alight on our cove split with rocks—

but I was not allowed to swim
beyond the jutting wreck
of ancient Vikings yet.

At twilight when
lime-green luna moths,
cecropia, polyphemus, sphinx,
their frightening eyes on wings blind hoax,
would waft through open panes
toward candles, sugared beer
and chloroform,

I was dreaming of you.

TASTING THE NAMES

Run your long fingers dry over those moist names:
Singosari, Singapura, Kuala Trengganu, Sumatra, Surabaya.
Laudanum names, papaya names strewn with peppercorn seeds.

At the volcano edge a ripening moon
frills as a flower in a Japanese shell
unfurls surprise in a water glass.

Plumes of forest pheasant twirl in a diadem
falsetto street operas, gamelans, chimes.
Whisper of cobras. New constellations

gong nightlong on the glistening beach
tracked by gravid sea turtles. Ambivalent
water buffalo poise between padi and path.

Shall I lead you into my ginger jungle
among blue fungi and indigo moths?
No trail of crumbs nor unravelled string.

Singosari. Singapura, Surabaya. Surabaya . . .
Laterite dust. Citrus sun. Monsoon.
Parang blades sharpen on stone.

A CIRCLE OF STONES

alone on the beach
the print of one foot
as if a man-bird
stepped in the wet
of a briny pond
the tide kept
filling and draining
while everyone slept
beyond the sea's reach
the man-bird leapt
toes in the foam
with a message unspooling
on whale-rib bones
he would not teach
but I overheard

A GIFT OF SEA SHELLS

Not diamonds, gold,
nor silver clasps,

nor could I catch
the shadow of the dolphin

who unzips the sea
at 4:00 o'clock, re-zips,

or the claw print
of a pelican upon the waves,

the egret's double
snowy in the pond,

nor keep hinged
the half-inch pair

of angel-wings
(what union stays

a perfect one?)
I send what perfect shells

I found for you today.
They may smash en route.

Unwashed, the bits
still taste the sea

and all our lives
and loves.

FORCES, VOICES

Locked in the vise
matrix of sandstone
the fossil scallop struggles
centuries in silence

only the sea speaks
as it beats beige rock
against the shore
also trying to free

grain from flute
shell from rock
ancient pectin from
contingent immortality

A JAPANESE MORNING

caught in mists of scrim
we wake beside an invisible sea

fog hides dock   apple orchard   Georgia pines
veils deer among plum trees and quince

as fog enshrouds the Budda at Kamakura
hides snow and sapphire around Fujiyama

this must be the inland sea
where teams of cormorants   dive

leashes around their throats   dive and dive
bring fish to masters crouched in skiffs

through fog on the sickle of sand
a crane proclaims longevity

or is he our heron patrolling tidewater
we know his croak he lifts across swamp

wisp by wisp the tardy sun
burns the day clear

over our flat slate cove
and briny Chesapeake

BATHERS, DUNNINGFORD COVE

Our nakedness may shock
neighbors across the cove
do they notice clothes on dock

muskrat dens beneath the shaky sod
soft underbelly of the marsh
holes trips us up

like muskrat pups we cavort
float bellies to the sun
they think no one sees   we do

must learn from muskrats how
to dive and swim and glory in
this briny water and ourselves

not shiver, cloaked, masked, safe, dry
awake all night, agonized
about the world beyond this cove

MEMENTO

Like a greedy lady octopus
I keep your gift within
long after your arms uncling
long after you jet away
through humid seas
leaving me in wet sun
among the seaweed strands

I'll bear you angel fish,
anemones with tawny tentacles,
freckled cowries,
scallops waving bright blue eyes
sea horses with auburn manes

When you regenerate again,
pull me from sea urchins, star fish, crabs,
strangle me with your entangling arms
I will enfold your want within
till it is mine
and squeeze my briny muscle rings
until you yield

FOR A
  CLINICAL
    SURVEY INQUIRING
      ABOUT
        FIRST
          LOVES

But *every* new love is the first!
All at first sight, *coup de foudre*.
Each unexpected, unique.

A generous spirit pleases the Lord,
or so I was raised,
minus details.

I lost my virginity
over and over again
in my adulterous brain.

The verb to love has no past tense—
wrote Konstantin Simonov, i.e.,
if it's genuine love, it lasts for life.

And beyond. Old lovers
hover in my life forever,
return as muses, amorous ghosts.

And, like the child at the rain-draped pane,
(every book in the house read thrice,
puzzles and games missing too many parts),

I keep watch: a new love might stop,
call "Come out, we still can explore,
beyond puddles, sun *will* shine again."

YOU ASK IF I'VE MET THE FAMOUS WRITER

I've yet to meet him in the flesh
but yes, I intend to read him.

Should we meet corporeally I will
caress the lobes of his famous ears.

In the photograph on his dust jacket—
in my house, an apt adjective—

his Adonic profile shows only one ear:
was the other lost in a literary scuffle?

I'll trace my fingers over his lips
parted in half-smile (ironic?)

graze his skin hinting wrinkles of wisdom
around insightful eyes, surely sapphire,

then stroke that broad brow, hope
to stoke his furnace of inspiration.

When at last we meet in the flesh
we will fit together like a Chinese

three-dimensional puzzle, all parts
interlocked, surface continuous, smooth . . .

But I was always impatient with puzzles,
though elderly aunts, to improve my mind,

brought them when I had a cold in the head.
I donated them all to the school bazaar.

So I fear in our passion we might insert
the wrong pieces in the wrong niches, concave

into convex, end up not as a sphere but a multi-armed
bodhisattva, or a Northwest Indian totem pole.

And what lurks below his dubious neck
may be lean and hard as a wooden puzzle,

as intricate and frustrating . . . Yet since
that's an old book, beneath his historic jaw

six chins may now reside, reservoirs of jowls
in chiaroscuro or five-o'clock shadow,

and, both flabby, we'd lump together
like bean bags or sacks of flour.

Or, like porcupines careless in love, we might
stick quills in each other's soft sectors.

What a gamut of juxtapositions
could flesh out our historic encounter!

Meanwhile, I promise to praise his books,
look out for him in the flesh . . .

PROPRIETARY CODES

You are my Harley-Davidson.

Old model, granted, a bit slow
on the uphill, uptake,
could use an overhaul, fresh paint.
Saddle's worn, I saw to that.

But tires good as new
though wheelies skid a bit.

In short, you still run okay.

And me, I got new leathers on,
slick and thick and black as tar,
boots with cleats, spike heels.

So I'm warning: any chick
tries to get a handle on you,
nick, scratch, stroke your fenders,
rev your motor,
jump astride—

you know the code:
One stray fingertip laid on—
I'd have to kill her.

I'll kill you too.

COMPANY

Found beneath the water-oak: one wren.
He lies belly up on my manuscripts tonight,
wire legs, beak a black thorn,
splash of daffodil above the tail—a fan of gray.

Below, three oblong patches, white.
Milkweed on his gold-stripped breast.
Wings wide—to applaud, or to escape?
Was he zapped in full song, full flight?

Toss a *bird* in the compost bin
with apple cores, orange rinds?
Compose/Compost . . . Quick—The door!
Clear up—What would guests say

of a host who keeps spent birds?
Mine's *not* a taste for moribund things,
but what can no longer sting,
peck, pierce or talk, I'll scrutinize.

Skulls are fine for saints to contemplate
(Mortality's an expected guest),
why not for a wingless sinner then
a cranium mere blueberry size?

OCCUPATION: AVIATOR

His stick has changed
into a cane!

He stabs dropped pears
wasp-studded in the café yard.

The August sun now warms
no more than his dim topaz glass.

Still, he rises, silver into blue,
leapfrogs mountains through the fog,

spears the bouncing sun, stars
targeted correctly, spirals higher—

Beneath his altitude
the sea shrinks to a pond.

The meteors mislead, charts
appear to map some other land,

stars prick out constellations
of unfamiliar hemispheres.

The engine clinks.
Wing lips ice.

The compass whirls, degrees
fall out, struts crack—

Who could cruise on course
or fly against such snow?

He would choose to crash,
cannot take off.

DIRECTIONS TO THE BOAT

Walk through the soy bean field
to the locust trees—you'll know
by the fragrance you're there—
push through bayberries, briars,
turn left by the foxes' den
onto the sickle of beach.

The keel grooves deep into the sand,
ospreys nest up the mast,
morning glories spiral the rigging,
eel grass sprouts between planks,
wasps paper hives under the bow,
mice tat sails into lace.

A decade ago, I promised you a sail.
Then you died. Still, we will travel:
the rudder steers straight, compass
points true, I've kept my old charts.
While you wait, please study the sky,
watch for any shift in the stars.

AMANDA CONTEMPLATES THE DUCK BLIND

Pity the dingy is beached nowadays so high above the tide line
but I'll drag her to the water, pole out, meet you once more—
Do you hear through the fog the channel marker bell?

How many sunsets we've sailed to your duck blind on stilts,
trailed lines so we seem to fish . . . and snagged a sturgeon
to scale and cook on your flotsam bucket stove before
the hours on sail bags, languid, tarpaulins a tent above.
Summers, eels battled to enter our minnow traps alive.
Autumn, strings of decoys floated from the blind.
We never shot a bird, but guarded nests all spring.
Winter, we tonged the shoal below the pilings, feasted on
oysters and one another. You called me Venus on Her Half-Shells,
said, Amanda is Latin for *she who must love*. Or was it *must be loved*?

Ancient barnacles coat the hull, gone are mast and boom and oars.
One hundred now, a shipless, shiftless captain wrecked ashore,
I again stand naked on sharp shells, prepare to dive.

INFOLDING

Tangier Island, Chesapeake Bay

Our dead sleep in our yards
between the rose hedge and the butane tank
beneath imported slabs and plastic glads,

and when, in our white boats
with stubby spines for keels, we churn
past empty sheds on pilings, tolling buoys,

we pass above clay graves below the grassy flat
or fuming seas which vomit spume and jellyfish
and sometimes granddads, brothers, cousins, sons.

We are a close-knit bit of land
and ravel in before the dark
through skinny channels dredged from shoals,

holds full of fish and crabs and eels,
surround ourselves with fog and night and sea
and with our families' souls.

FIRE WORKS: CHRONICLES FROM A WAR

1.
when fires were ignited
entire congregation inside
nobody thought to smsh
the fine stained glass

heavy doors were locked
buttressed with bales of hay
people assured each other *here
we are safe for a while*

men in the hills
binoculars trained
on flashes of flame
tornados of smoke

heard bugles blasts drums
thought *fireworks*
and cheered the end
of the war

they ran to the valley
to find the priest
tied to a tomb in the yard
and left to repeat

psalms for the parish inside
his left hand free to swing
the incense lamp
which torched the hay

gone mad amid rubble shards
embers cooled in three days
the men bore the blame
for their lack of surrender

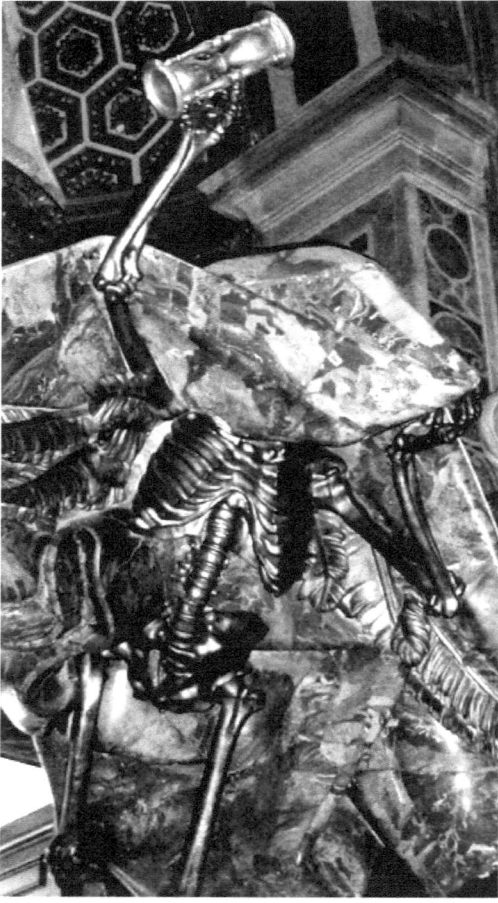

which might not after all
have saved the town
they filtered off to ports
where men were in short supply

2.
not virgin troops but trained
the soldiers marched on
to a village stocked with wine
barrels of beer   girls to serve

one soldier took his own life
another transferred to the front
some drank till they died
others reached homes in far lands

and mothers children and wives
begot babies reopened shops worked farms
attended christenings weddings and wakes
and tried to forget

3.
perhaps while most in the town
were herded inside the church
one boy and one girl up to no good
slipped through the woods to a cave

like animals sensed
Too Dangerous to Return
lived on berries and nuts
began a new clan

perhaps that wasn't a church but
temple or mosque or school a
different war or land or time but
this is how it was   how it is

FORGET I GAVE YOU ANCESTORS TO DIE FOR

Forget I gave you ancestors to die for,
their portraits, medals, multicolored ribbons framed
high on my wall—all yours someday.

Certain uncles lie on foreign fields, heroic and
unmarked, where no potatoes grow and children play,
their bones the same as those who merely served, or fled.

Forget I early taught you to be brave,
face all one does in childhood and beyond.
you do not want that plot in Arlington too soon.

Forget you are a woman, made babies like the ones
you think you save. What woman's meant to fight
in combat zones? Most wars are all around.

But you will go where you are told, regardless right
or wrong, tell others when their time to disembark.
So this is yours.

LUCKIES TASTE GOOD!

danced through my brain
and *like a cigarette should!*
pirouetted across my lips.

I'd walk a mile for a camel—
didn't know those belching humps
up-chucked, kicked, and smelled.

I'd thought to please her for once.
She'd studied poetry, French,
played Chopin and Bach,

worked hard, fought for pay
high as a man's. Ashtrays dumped
twice a day overflowed . . . Vodka bottles—

I called for *Phillip Morris* until
my mother muttered *damns*
no child should hear.

"Whoever wrote that jingle, dear,
a penniless poet, rhymester for hire,
should have used, *as*, not *like*."

Yet the Lucky Strike I filched
from her purse did *not* after all
Mean Fine Tobacco. Cured me.

She loved her cylinders of white,
at 67 died: a heart attack,
You tell me now, "That jingle was

for *Winstons*, didn't she know
they butcher grammar to make
everyone buy? She did."

THE SAINT IN A BOX OF GLASS

She keeps calling out to me
in Old Church Slavonic *Release!*

Let me out and I will reveal
only to you the martyrdoms

of all three saints whose name
you bear but have no hope

to emulate. Know
what you will miss.

Her promises are dimmed
as fish songs in aquariums.

Brush my hair, please,
it keeps on growing—

Tangles glow amber
in the murky cathedral.

Bend down, kiss my holy bones.
Mine are stronger than your own.

I buy and light a taper, drip
hot wax on a brass tray, stick
one end in the puddle till it holds,
then glance over my shoulder.

She seems to twitch.
I flee beyond the walls.

CONJECTURES IN A SMALL CEMETERY BEYOND THE NO-FRILLS MICROTEL

Death hasn't taken *these* away
but brought them here, the clan
reunion in a consecrated patch
beside a February field where

last fall's soy bean stalks whisker
the upturned ground, rich
in history and nitrogen,
North Carolina, exit 121 off I-95.

The only neighbor, 86, owned the land,
still tends the cemetery, shows where
she will lie beside her soldier man
beneath this bare black walnut tree

and the five crepe-myrtle skeletons stretch
over her sisters. Dogwood boughs, bridal white,
hover like angels above the hamlet markers.
She plunks a pot of her handmade poinsettias

before a granite cross marked DAVIS. Here
plaques read Eva *1865-1933*; Edward Paul,
1921, joined Army '41, died of age not war
in 1993; and Ruby Lee, a wife, 1927-1984.

A son still plants that field in beans.
They sold their other land for six motels
and Cracker Barrel Family Restaurant
(kids welcome, scrumptious cakes, no booze).

In graveyards one is meant to meditate upon
mortality, whether it's enough to have lived,
to find wisdom and metaphors, then compose
elegies to these comfortable strangers.

Lonely stones in other fields call me. *My soldier* ancestors,
Scattered. Their lives are inside mine, no need for wreaths
or requiems. Still, they summon, each from his terrain.
I tear the crabgrass from these slabs, and leave.

FOR
A
CERTAIN
POET
IN
PRISON

When you die
who can close
your eyes

they tried
to silence
your lips

but your ears
record footsteps
of roaches and soldiers

smashed finger tips
translate specks
into syllables

the thought
of a bird
into song

your eyes will
never shut   dead
you still dream

NIGHT SHIFT

A shift of light
at the edge of
earth   how to catch
that rim of light gold
ring or brass no
matter   light
a beacon   sign
I cannot catch
not meant to catch
and still I try
and still   will try

EXISTENTIAL QUESTIONS

1.
On living or dying.
This time, 1973, the mushrooms, alabaster
parasols of death in sour cream,

after a September afternoon of poems and guitar,
motorcycles revving behind the stage, and later
forbidden tasting beyond the floating dock,

then feet mud-caked dashing from car to woods
the whole trip to vomit beyond the dark road—
The start of pain, the ritual sense of doom,

the midnight agony of cramps through legs
and pelvis, then chest squeezed by a closing vise,
while in the Sibley E.R., interns not yet

trained for fungal toxins, ask and ask,
Can you name the current president?
I recount the blunders of his reign.

At 2 a.m., wheeled to bed, sixth floor,
the night nurse asks in her Georgia voice sultry
with cinders and dark velvet gladiolas,

Honey, is there anythin' I kin git you?
Who'd dare say tea at this hour, ward
kitchen sprayed and locked?

She brings one Styrofoam cup,
an ambered string to a Lipton bag
more sacred than all the Oolong tins

clipper-shipped from India. Then
she fills a white enamel bowl and
washes my feet.

2.
Below Johns Hopkins Hospital, 2004, the street is gone:
trees, dead leaves, leaf-blowers, their noise, black bags,
ash cans, loose dogs, ants on October grass.

More questions, Decisions: easy as switching the power off?
Would have been, then. Plate shards, stored pills,
penknives, forgotten scissors, smashed glass?

Yet that life force . . . Or dumb habit, sloth, lack of bravado all
those unfinished tasks—and silly to skip out now
when so many are shipping out daily, unwilled.

Till the last tattle and rattle the crone, blind to her liver marks, the
old man despite aches and clocks, unresolved regrets,
cling or are clung to quotidian routines.

And one can't disappoint those who wrote notes, brought sweets,
sent bouquets, tried to phone. So, one does not.
For how will the book turn out?

VISIONS OF MY HALF-AWAKE

Peculiar actors inhabit this night
their dialogue dim-heard, half understood,
as I leap across beds, some occupied, or in.

The dramatis personae! Royal types
from six-foot decks of cards, trapezoidal head
gear flat red and gold and black, blend

to blobs, stretch into other characters.
One dame in thick green petticoats
hands me quilts, or clothes, though I

no longer dream my nakedness. Just
as well these days, though behind the scrim
I am the viewer, and not the viewed.

New troupes materialize, mutate, dissolve
to puddles, fade off stage. no way
to save them in formaldehyde . . .

Aware of all this masquerade,
I watch the carnival yet also dance . . .
Visions and visitors play

their airy roles, then waltz away
to new sets, stages out of range.
Let me stay within this world!

Pain and sunrise tug me out. Must wait
till I too am chimera, slated to appear/
disappear in someone else's lucid dream.

TIDAL QUESTIONS

The sea is a generous grave.
Inland, they describe
my dying but,

unaware, I
turned back. So
what could I tell?

Was I truly almost dead?
New currents collide.
Was dying as if

sucked out
by this rip tide
but saved in time?

A sudden tidal surge—
Sandpipers all survive,
know when to take wing.

CASE HISTORIES: YOU SAY I AM NOW ONE

One should at least bring back
a report from the Other Side.

Didn't Persephone describe Hades while
she shared that perilous pomegranate?

I nibble them too, seed by seed,
so far return, sticky with juice,

clothes awry, my scribbled notes
in sweet magenta ink.

My seasons still
recapitulate themselves:

summer, swallows transcribe the cove,
winter, the eagle replaces the osprey.

All year, gray fox and coon rewrite the fields,
great herons cross out dying suns.

Those insomniac nights the stars, reported
eternal, punctuate evergreen Georgia pines:

their charcoal lines record a dawn, feverish or anemic.
How much the medical journals ignore . . .

CHOREOGRAPHY

Not at the far side of the music but
caught in the vortex now
everything is mystery, surprise

I'm captured in a dance
not yet prefigured
and pattern unpredictable

I can't forehear the
notes and only know
they're new and intricate

But may they score
a graceful culmination
to this life of stumbling steps

Elisavietta Ritchie

Likened to Elizabeth Bishop, Marianne Moon and Anna Akhmatova before she had read them, twenty-six of Elisavietta Ritchie's books and chapbooks are in print, and hundreds of poems, stories, creative non-fiction, photographs, and translations from Russian, French and other languages have appeared in numerous publications in the United States and abroad, including *Poetry*, *The American Scholar*, *New York Times*, *Christian Science Monitor*, *Washington Post*, *National Geographic*, *JAMA: Journal of the American Medical Association*, and dozens of literary journals. Individual poems, stories and collections were winners or finalists in competitions. Her book *Flying Time* is the winner of four PEN Syndicated Fiction awards.

Ritchie's work is widely anthologized, and she created and edited anthologies. She has translated, edited and line-edited various works of fiction, poetry and non-fiction. She often teaches creative writing to adults and students, has served as president for fiction and for poetry for Washington Writers' Publishing House, founded The Wineberry Press, hosted a radio program interviewing poets and writers, consulted on various literary activities, and has devoted efforts to emerging, imprisoned and dissident writers.

She has read her works at such noted institutions as the Library of Congress, Harbourfront, Folger Library, Harvard and other universities, as well as at schools, libraries and other cultural centers in the United States and abroad. The United States Information Agency sponsored her readings in Brazil, the Far East, and the Balkans. Her poems have been translated into a dozen languages.

Her education includes The Sorbonne, Cornell University, University of California, Berkeley, American University (MA in French) and further studies at The Writer's Center, Bethesda, Toronto Martial Arts Commission, and The National Association for Poetry Therapy. Her life-long interests include the natural sciences, wildlife and marine conservation, sailing, history, languages, medicine and photography.

Ritchie's home base since 1959 is Southern Maryland and Washington, DC, but she grew up in various cities in the United States. She has lived in Malaysia, Cyprus, Lebanon, France, Canada and Australia, and travels extensively. She is married to Clyde Farnsworth, noted novelist and former *New York Times* correspondent, and has one daughter, two sons and two stepsons.

Donald G. Shomette

As a writer and historian Donald G. Shomette is the author of eighteen books on archaeology, history, and early American urban development, and thrice winner of the John Lyman Book Award for Best American Maritime History. His many academic and popular articles have appeared in such national publications as *National Geographic Magazine*, *History and Technology*, *Sea History* and *American Neptune*. He was the recipient of the Calvert Prize, Maryland's highest award for historic preservation, and an honorary Doctor of Humane Letters from the University of Baltimore for his contributions to the arts, science and letters. He has appeared in numerous documentaries on the History Channel, the Discovery Channel, the National Geographic Channel, NBC, CBS, PBS and the BBC.

As an award winning art director, graphic designer and photographer, he has served on the staffs of the Library of Congress, the *Washington Post*, and the *Wall Street Journal*. As a marine archaeologist he has worked throughout the United States, Western Europe, and Central America under the sponsorship of such organizations and agencies as the National Geographic Society, the National Park Service, the U.S. Navy, and a variety of educational and museological institutions. His travels as a lecturer, writer and researcher have taken him to no less than thirty-two countries in Europe, Africa, Central and South America. As a cultural resources manager he has served as a consultant for numerous states, various agencies of the U.S. government, museums and universities. He is currently CEO of Cultural Resources Management, and serves as advisor to the Mallows Bay National Marine Sanctuary Initiative.

Acknowledgments

Many of the poems in this manuscript are too recent to submit individually, but we wish to thank the editors of the publications in which a few of the older poems appeared, most in earlier versions.

"Bathers, Dunningford Cove," *The Broadkill Review*, issue 2, 2007; "Beyond the North Woods," as "Beyond Little Black River, Manitoba," *The Christian Science Monitor*, 1995; *The Arc of the Storm*, Signal Books, 1998; "Babushka's Beads," *Potomac Review*, 2007; "Case Histories," *Visions* 2006; "Choreography," *Salome, Moving to Larger Quarters*, 1982; *Finding the Name*, Wineberry Press, 1983; performed as theater piece in *The Poem Is The Last Resort*, created and directed by Jerilyn Gilstrap; "Clinical Survey Inquiring About First Loves," Nancy Kalish, Ph.D., www.lostlovers.com;" Directions to the Boat," *Confrontation, Awaiting Permission to Land*, 2006; "Eternal as Turtles," *Wetlands*; *Tightening The Circle Over Eel Country*, Acropolis Books, 1974; "For A Certain Poet in Prison," *Awaiting Permission to Land*, Cherry Grove Collections, 2006; "Forces, Voices," as "Impasse," 1974, *The Christian Science Monitor*; *Tightening The Circle Over Eel Country*, Acropolis Books, 1974; "Forget I Gave You Ancestors to Die For:" *Bombshells: War Stories and Poems by Women on the Homefront*, Missy Martin, Jesse Loren, eds., Omniarts Press, 2007; "Flotsam, Jetsam," *Blue Unicorn*, 2007; "Infolding, Tangier Island," *Tightening The Circle Over Eel Country*, Acropolis Books, 1974; "Luckies Taste Good!" *K.I.S. & Your Butts Goodbye*, George J. Pearce III, ed., 2007; "Memento," *Epoch*, 1969+-; *Tightening The Circle Over Eel Country*, 1974; "Moon Pursuit," *Tightening The Circle Over Eel Country*, 1974; "Navigational Problems," *The Broadkill Review*, issue 2, 2007; "Occupation: Aviator," *A Sheath of Dreams And Other Games*, Proteus Press, 1976; "On Weathering Gales," *The Christian Science Monitor*; *Raking The Snow*, Washington Writers Publishing House, 1982, *The Lake Ontario Log*, 1994, *More Golden Apples* and *American Sports Poems*, Papier Mache Press; "Osprey," *Ann Arbor Review*, 2004; "Ours Is An Untidy Earth," www.PoemsfortheTsunamiVictims.org. reprinted in *Only The Sea Keeps*, Sankar Roy and Judith Robinson, eds., Bayeaux Press, 2005; "Prefigurations," as "For A Certain Artist," *Heal Your Soul, Heal The World*, June Cotner, ed., Andrews McMeel Press, 1999; *Looking or God in All the Right Places: Prayers and Poems to Comfort, Inspire, and Connect Humanity*, June Cotner, ed.,Loyola Press, October 2003; set to choral music by composer David L. Brunner, premiered 2005. Boosey & Hawkes, music publishers, New York; "Proprietary Codes," *Earth's Daughters /Take Me To Your Leader*, issue 62, 2003, "Poem of the Month"; "Real Toads," *Confrontation*, (2007); "Siren Summer," *A Sheath of Dreams And Other Games*; "Swimmer," *The Christian Science Monitor*, 1981; *Out of Season*, Amaganssett Press, 1992; "Tasting the Names," *Poetry Now*; in Indonesian and Malay, in *Berita Buana*, 1977, *Budaya Jaya*, 1978; *Raking The Snow*; "Visions of my Half-Awake:" *Visions*, 2006; "Wineberries," "Great Uncle Ramsey" *Full Moon*, 1970; "You Ask If I've Met The Famous Writer," *Second Glance*, 1994; *Elegy For The Other Woman*, Signal Books, 1996.

www.ingramcontent.com/pod-product-compliance
Lightning Source LLC
Chambersburg PA
CBHW041819080526
44587CB00005B/145